MW00632722

WALKING with DOGS

A SPIRITUAL JOURNEY.

To Eileen

With Blessings and hugs

Marti Healy

MARTI HEALY

Illustrations by Mimi Durand Caroe

Mimi Durand Caroe

Copyright © 2017 Marti Healy

All rights reserved. No part of this book may be used or reproduced in any manner whatsoever without prior permission from the publisher.

ISBN 978-0-9857018-4-0

First Edition

Printed in China

Illustrations © 2017 Mimi Durand Caroe

Published by The Design Group Press, LLC
www.thedesigngrouppress.com

Author contact: www.martihealybooks.com

Dedicated To
All The Dogs Who Have
Walked With Me.

COME WALK WITH US:
An Invitation.

I don't remember when I first realized that walking with dogs
was a spiritual journey for me. Now, of course,
I understand it has always been so.

I think I noticed initially that I seemed to be "in prayer" a great deal while I was walking with dogs. Not praying as such, but *in* prayer.
I have read somewhere that having a "prayer partner" can be a good thing. I am blessed with two at the moment. One is a gorgeous redhead, with ears that flop and a rump that swaggers and a coat that glistens in the sunlight. She is about 54 pounds, a mix of great proportions – from golden retriever to border collie, with a bit of chow thrown in to make things interesting. She is Sophie.

The other partner is soft-spoken and shy. Although he stands a bit taller than, and weighs about the same as, Sophie, he bows to her every whim and lead. He is utterly devoted to her and me (in that order). He is black and brown and leans toward the German shepherd family, with large, black, almond-shaped eyes that can laugh with joy or break your heart. He is Teddy.

Both are foundlings. God put them in my path, and I am ever so grateful.

Sophie and Teddy and I walk together almost every day. We are surrounded with an amazing assortment of wondrous walking opportunities.

In the heart of our town, there is a huge, dense, ancient forest where the stillness is absolute, and we whisper to each other.

Nearby is a formal gardens with fountains and duck ponds and turtles, a mystical labyrinth, canopies of giant trees, and paths of brick and dirt underfoot.

Within a few blocks, we can enter a primeval tangle of woods that surrounds a natural body of water. It is called a "Carolina Bay" and is one of just a few to be found in the world. (Scientists think the Carolina Bay dates back to the time of the dinosaurs. Sophie, Teddy and I, on the other hand, know for a fact it was created by fairies.)

In addition to these fabulous walking places, we live on the very edge of a residential district that has foregone paved streets for the benefit of the horses who live there. This horse district has a heritage that gives priority to the animals over all other considerations. There are carriages and riders and horses of every description. There are paddocks and stables and race tracks and polo fields – all open to the walking dog as well.

This is a Southern town, with weather that is as gracious and welcoming as its people. This is a town that loves its animals – dogs in particular. And we are privileged to walk almost daily through this paradise. How could I not find it a spiritual journey?

And yet, I believe walking with dogs in any environment can potentially have this effect for each of us. If our hearts are open. If our souls are watchful. If our faith is receptive. We need only to follow the lead of the dogs at our side.

Come walk with us.

In The Company Of Dogs.

It's 7:00 a.m. No alarm has gone off. My eyes are shut tightly.
I can't see a clock. But I am quite aware that it is 7:00 a.m.

It's the undeniable sound of doggy toenails clicking on the hardwood floor at either side of my bed that gives me the only clue I need.

If I lie very still and keep my breathing even, they may decide to discreetly walk away and grant me another 15, 30, or even 60 minutes of sleep. It depends on their mood. But they will be back.

For all their size and energy, Sophie and Teddy, my beloved mixed-breed canine companions, are quite easygoing about this morning ritual. There is no barking, no jumping on the bed, no licking my face. Just toenails clicking as they pace on tiptoe back and forth, back and forth, to determine if I am ready yet. I think it's the invitational aspect of it that finally urges me up. Who could deny the pleasure of being asked to join them for the highlight of their day? Our morning walk.

Kindly, they don't seem to care how I look or what I wear. I find the first thing I can to throw on. They hurry to the back door, dancing and nipping playfully at each other in anticipation of the strapping on of collars.

This summer, they've taught themselves to "hydrate" well before we start – even as I'm filling their water bottle to take along. We've been trying to walk earlier, before the real heat of the day. But this summer has become a challenge – and we walk from shade to shade, down earth-packed roads, along the edges of open fields, through stands of thick old trees. But not one of us would consider calling off the walk on account of weather.

Even though we start out at varying times, we typically encounter many of the same friends who are also out for their morning ritual. There's Pongo, Scraps, Sally and Sukie, Rags, Patches, sometimes Annie and Harry, Buddy on weekends, and others. Their human companions greet us with smiles and friendship just as warm and genuine as those on four feet (or three, in Pongo's case).

This summer, for the very first time, Sophie and Teddy are allowed off leash while we are on the polo practice field. Sophie revels in the new-found freedom and space, leaping and rolling, running flat out, lolling in a mud-puddle, but not taking advantage of the trust she instinctively understands. Teddy fights back long-ago abandonment issues, but loves the "meet and greet" with the other dogs. He does his best to stay near me, trotting to keep up. Watching me for reassurance. Watching Sophie constantly.

When we take our leave, we travel most of the way back home alone. And it is during this phase of the morning walk that I realize the deepest pleasure. The best part of the journey. It is the solitude. The companionable silence. No need for words. No need for anything.

It seems to me that only walking with dogs can we know this experience so honestly. Only walking with dogs does it come so naturally.

Sometimes, we may hum a little tune. Sometimes, we may stop to examine a new sight or smell, a small flower or a funny stick. Sometimes, Sophie halts and sits, looking at me expectantly, and I know it's time for a drink.

We stop and rest on a rock sometimes. We wave to passersby. But, for the most part, we are silent. In the moment. In thought. Listening. This is my time to be in prayer. I suspect it may be the same for Sophie and Teddy as well. I invite God to join us. And we all seem to feel his presence.

Mother Teresa once said, "God is the friend of silence." So are dogs, I think. And I quite believe that God is definitely the friend of peaceful morning walks, in silence, in the company of dogs.

Relinquishing The Lead.

At the northwest entrance, the red brick walkway
lies long and straight ahead of us.

The pathway is several feet wide and bordered on both sides by thick cool seas of dark ivy. Fat lumpy trunks of cypress and oak and magnolia spread upward out of the lush green beds, lifting a high arching bridgework of limbs over our heads.

As we pass through the iron gates of the city's public gardens, the dogs hurry their pace. We have a sort of agreement here. Here, they are allowed to take the lead.

The brick pathways branch and lace in all directions throughout the gardens. Occasional dirt-packed or graveled or old stone walks also crisscross them at various points.

These unending trails seem to go everywhere and nowhere. They are clearly evident and easy to wander. So I let Sophie and Teddy choose which turn we will take, which way we will follow. They understand instinctively, and tug with enthusiasm on their leashes, as if they were reined to a wagon.

Back and forth, east and west, north and south, up and down, forward and over and back again. Across bridges and under trellises; along the edges of the gentle ponds and streams filled with nosey fish and shy turtles.

We stop to watch the ducks, who pretend very hard not to notice us. The squirrels see us coming, wait tantalizingly, then scoot chuckling up a tree. We relish every new sight and scent.

Rarely, Teddy will choose one way, while Sophie selects another. But they unanimously agree soon enough, and I don't usually have to break the tie. Some kind of negotiation takes place, but I can't really read it. A canine form of "rock-scissors-paper" perhaps.

Eventually, I have to take the lead back, of course. When it's time to leave and go home. But I think I enjoy this lead-reversal as much as they do. It takes me down pathways I might not have traveled. It stops me to relish a moment. It delights me to see how Sophie and Teddy think and react and cooperate with each other.

My mind fills with images of walking in a garden with God. As a child, one of my favorite hymns was "I Come to the Garden Alone." It still is. I remember being in awe of the possibility that God would choose to walk with me – in a personal, one-of-a-kind relationship. I reveled in the image of it being early morning – with dew and roses and stillness. And, even back then, I saw at least one dog walking with us, too.

I wonder if these walks in this garden with Sophie and Teddy are practices for garden walks with God. Does God let me have the lead there with Him? Does He enjoy where I take Him? Does He delight in my presence and listening to me and learning how I think and feel and relate to my fellow human beings? Or, perhaps, it is the opposite lesson that I am meant to be learning. A very different example being set. Am I being shown how to let go of the lead? Giving my will over to God? Seeing where He will lead me?

Thinking back on the song, there is no real clue. God and I are simply walking together. He walks with me. He talks with me. He tells me I am His own. It even goes on to say that the joy we feel is a "shared" one. And uniquely ours.

The joy I share with Sophie and Teddy is also one-of-a-kind. With fellowship and love. With appreciation for all the earthly gifts God has given us to enjoy. Regardless of who is leading whom, I suspect we are, somehow, following a way God wants us to go.

Wait.

"Sophie, wait!" I command. The words are hoarse and hissed,
just above a whisper. There is an urgency to them.

I can see the carriage horses approaching. But from Sophie's low, four-legged vantage point, I know they are out of her view.

Sophie slows and hesitates. But then begins to creep ahead. She'll take off running again, I know. I know the body language. She's not looking at me. Only the squirrel. Only the squirrel racing idiotically – hypnotically – around the base of a tree on the opposite side of the road.

"Sophie … *wait!*" I try to let her hear my seriousness of tone. But I must keep my volume low because of the approaching horses. If she ignores my command, if she darts out through the bushes and across the road as she is headed, she will be directly in the path of the four horses and the carriage they are pulling. Startled, the horses could bolt. They could rear and cause unthinkable damage to themselves and the riders. They could crush Sophie herself. This is real danger. She must obey.

"Sophie … *WAIT! … SIT!*" Once more, she slows. This time, she stops. She sits. She obeys.

The knot in my stomach eases as I reach her side. Clipping her leash back onto her collar I praise her for her obedience. The carriage driver nods and calmly passes by.

Walking with dogs in the horse district is beautiful, but sometimes challenging. Especially when trying to allow the dogs a bit of freedom off leash. I try to stagger the times, to avoid the highest potential for crossing paths with these magnificent animals – who do, after all, have priority and right-of-way.

But Sophie's spirit and energy and intelligence coax me into taking the chance of off-leash privileges. As long as she follows my commands, all is well. It's her independent-mindedness – her exercise of free will – that I find so fearful.

My other walking canine companion – Teddy – is another story altogether. Teddy has abandonment issues. Teddy wants me to metaphorically hold his hand at all times. Ted is most secure when attached to me by leash and I am leading the way.

I wonder which I am most like in the eyes of God. I suspect I am more like Sophie than I would care to admit. I suspect I obey primarily when it suits me. And I also rather readily admit that one of the hardest commands for me to follow is "wait."

Perhaps this is because from my vantage point on earth and in life I am sublimely oblivious to the "danger" from which God may be trying to protect me. Why should I wait? I am chasing something terribly compelling. I want it now. But God may see the idiocy of my quest. The danger to myself and others. The bigger picture.

Perhaps he just needs me to practice obedience. To forego my self-seeking free will for his perfect wisdom.

God often whispers "wait." Will I be wise enough to unquestioningly and immediately obey?

Perhaps today, Sophie has taught me well.

Letting Go.

New Year's Eve. "Come on Sophie, go out for a long one!"

It's a warm, soft day. Sophie, Teddy and I have stopped at the polo practice field to have a quick game of catch.

For the most part, Sophie is the one who goes after the ball. Teddy is just learning this art. So we throw a few short ones out to him. Sophie graciously lets him have his turn. But he readily defers to her the better part of the time.

Sophie loves playing ball. Well, most of it. She loves the throwing part, the chasing part, the catching part, even the returning part. But then there's the "letting go" part. Not so easy. You can see it in her eyes – she wants so much to enjoy the whole experience again, but just can't make herself let go of the ball to enable it to be re-thrown.

Somewhere, a long time ago, I remember reading that the only fear we humans are born with is the fear of falling. I always found that interesting – the idea that we apparently have to be taught all of our other fears. Upon closer thought, however, I wonder if we could more accurately reclassify that inherent fear of falling as the fear of "letting go." (Typically, if you don't let go, you don't fall.)

This idea actually began to form in my mind after a very small and self-centered occurrence a week or so ago: I got my hair cut. I finally said "good-bye" to a long-familiar part of myself in the form of a 10-inch ponytail. Admittedly, something as trivial as getting one's hair cut shouldn't be a life-altering experience. But it did make me more aware of this whole frightening thing of "letting go."

Most of us can look in the backs of our closets and the bottoms of our sock drawers and in at least one of our desk drawers and relate to that feeling of not being able to "let go" of those small tangible bits of our lives.

There are, of course, much larger "letting go" issues in life. Saying good-bye to loved ones, to homes we have known, to friends who no longer share our daily experience.

Other fears of "letting go" may be more obscure: I think part of the reason why I'm carrying around a bit of extra weight is that I just don't want to "let go" of the enjoyment of eating. Who wants to let go of chocolate? Or Christmas cookies? I also don't look forward to the idea of letting go of the comfort of sitting on the sofa and watching old movies.

Last Christmastime in church, our minister talked about the gifts that the wisemen brought to the baby Jesus. She compared the gifts to those we can still offer up in our faith today. She suggested that those gifts of the old kings could be translated into modern-day terms to mean everything from personal talents to old grudges.

What a lovely new way of looking at "letting go," I thought. Gather up all that talent and ability you've been saving, and let it go out as a wonderful gift to the world. Pool together your love and affection, and let it go to wash over someone who needs it. Acknowledge an old grudge or hurt, stop protecting and polishing it, and just let it go.

I try to help Sophie get over her fear of letting go by offering her a second ball every time she returns the first one. You can't enjoy a spiffy new ball experience without letting go of the old one, we're learning.

I'm thinking my new short haircut now deserves a buff new body under it. So maybe letting go of the ponytail will turn out to be the first step in letting go of the cookies (but please, not all of the chocolate) and at least some of the time on the couch.

I'll do what I can with the talent thing. Hugs have never been hard for me to "let go" of, so I'll just have to keep that up. Hurts to my heart, my ego, my pride, I've decided I'll take to the edge of the old year, and then just let go.

But I suspect that letting go of the fear of letting go will be the most freeing experience of all. After all, according to the experts, I've been carrying that one around with me since birth.

A Gift Of Sticks.

I have a lap full of sticks. There are seven of them.

One stick is quite large and handsomely mottled with turquoise-colored mold on its outer bark. Others are mere twigs – deep brown, still supple. One even still sports its leaves – although they are curled and dried and crumble to the touch. All of them are treasured gifts. All have been brought to me with care, one at a time, by Sophie.

Today, at the conclusion of our walk, Sophie and Teddy and I have opted to sit out on the back steps awhile before we go inside. One of God's perfect days. Just warm enough. Cool breezes. Birds and squirrels and cats to entertain us.

But sitting quietly is not often an option for young Sophie. And so, for some reason known only to her own heart, she has chosen this peaceful time to gather and present me with sticks.

Sticks have long been her gifts of choice. She periodically brings them inside to me at all hours of the day and night and drops them carefully into my lap or at my feet or beside my bed. Sometimes she waits politely for me to notice her sitting in front of me with one protruding from her mouth. I thank her abundantly, receive it with admiration, and she leaves happily to go do other important dog things.

I remember when Sophie began this practice. She was just a baby. And her gifts were given then only to her littermate, Maggie. I had found both young abandoned puppies at the side of a road just outside of town. Maggie was so much smaller, quieter. Soon, she became weak and fragile, unable to grow. She blessed my life for only a few short weeks. Toward the end, Sophie would bring Maggie these earthly gifts every time she went outside. The only way she knew to say, "I love you. Please get well. Please don't leave us."

But Maggie did leave us. And Sophie and I grieved together, even as we struggled to find our own bond. Then, one very special day, Sophie brought a stick to *me*. They have been our secret love notes ever since.

There are times – especially after a storm or strong winds – when I can hear a series of sharp banging noises, followed by rather alarming scraping and cracking and rustling sounds, and I am alerted to the fact that a good-sized branch is most likely being dragged in through the doggy door on my behalf. I suspect this may have more to do with Sophie expressing her sense of humor than her affection. But it is handed over with pride just the same.

For months now, I have been worried about my gifts to God. They are so meager, I feel. Church and charities. Time and talents. Not much treasure. Of what worth are they in God's eyes, I fret? And yet, looking down now into my lap, I know that Sophie's sticks touch my heart deeply. Do I think I am so much more sensitive – so much more loving and understanding – than God?

I know that in dog culture, the stick itself is unimportant. It is the act of giving that holds all the significance. The sharing. The passing of joy, one to another. I know, too, that it must not be given back. To have it accepted is a great part of its meaning.

Perhaps when I evaluate my gifts to God in such a light they take on a different look. A bit of shine. A new glow. Perhaps I should just offer the stick, and let God decide the value.

On yet another level, perhaps they represent my gifts *from* God. My gifts of the spirit. Do I use them all to their fullest extent – great and small, fresh and supple, or broken and crumbling, crashing through the doorway with delight, or dropped delicately at the very feet of God? Do I know their worth?

Sophie does not seem to spend much time on choosing just the right gift for me. She brings whatever she has. It is her prize. And she gives it freely and joyfully.

And so I gather up Sophie's sticks from my lap, take them inside, and put them in a glass vase in the morning sun on the ledge of my kitchen window.

And I wonder if perhaps my own gifts – my meager words of worship, the humble sticks collected along my spiritual journey – are tucked safely in a vase, in the sun, in God's kitchen window.

Waiting With The Crane.

The ancient, gray skeleton might never have come to light,
had it not been for the excessive drought this past year.

Not of human origin – or even animal or bird or amphibian – the bare bones and underbelly of our beloved Carolina Bay have been mercilessly, frighteningly exposed.

Tucked away on the southern edge of town, the Carolina Bay is a favorite walking place for the dogs and me. It stunned us to see this lovely spot so barren and suffering and vulnerable.

I knew the Bay itself was becoming more and more shallow over the past weeks and months without any meaningful rains. But I was not prepared for the empty reality that greeted us on this day's walk.

It had been awhile. And, like visiting an old friend who has been struggling with issues of health or other life stresses – a friend you haven't seen for much too long – the change made me catch my breath.

The dogs' senses sharpened, nosing the ground, looking around in every direction.

The lone, large, resident crane was still there. Standing regally and aloof as always. But, today, he was out in the very center of the Bay. Posed erect on a mound of smooth gray clay that jutted unexpectedly into the air.

I had never seen this island before; it had always been well beneath the water's surface. Only a few segregated areas of ponding water remain. Enough to still reflect some of the flaming reds and golds of the trees that surround the Bay, holding it in refuge.

It is usually one of the awesomely beautiful autumn panoramas I look forward to. But, today, the greater part of the Bay's surface is now undulating gray earth. In some places, a soft covering of green grass-like growth sprouts up. It looks a bit like the delicate strands that typically wave across the floor of a wild pond. Young spring in color. Hard to place. Out of place.

In other areas, where the clay has dried and is beginning to harden, there are a few footprints – both animal and human. Perhaps they crept forward into this foreign ground out of curiosity. Perhaps, as fellow mourners, they came to pay their respects.

I remember when I first saw this Carolina Bay walking with Sophie alone. It was before Teddy had even come to live with us. It took my breath away then, too. But for entirely different emotions.

It had been a very wet season then. The Bay was at its peak of intriguing, natural loveliness. Full of life. The water was like a liquid mirror, reflecting the sky and branches of its forest, rippling from small life forms within and above. Birds gathered to praise it. Creatures hovered near it with sounds of delight. It was pure magic. Created and inhabited by fairies, Sophie and I concluded. She explored and reveled in it with puppy enthusiasm. Now – today – the fairies seem to be in hiding; hauntingly absent. The birds are silent. No ripples dip the small, dead pools. Only the lone crane waits.

Even the sky has begun to shed a light mist of grief over this almost forsaken place. Sophie suddenly jerks up her head in anticipation. But it is only a fallen leaf tumbling uninterrupted across the open space.

The mist has grown heavier with promise now. It clings in tiny droplets on the needles of the pine trees. It makes the gray floor slick and shine. Perhaps there is hope for its reclamation, I pray in my heart. For all the living things that have loved and left here, I pray for the rain in my heart.

I know that the Carolina Bays are millions and millions of years old. I know they have survived countless droughts and floods and years of erosion and the interference of man for generation after generation after generation. I know that this, too, shall pass. It will be reborn. And, even in its altered state, it is somehow incredibly, compellingly, lovely still. It continues to be a place of awesome beauty.

Sophie and Teddy and I will try to be hopeful and wait. We'll wait for our secret sanctuary to come back to us. My soul searches and drifts and comes to rest on the symbolism of waiting for Christ's return. The ultimate sanctuary.

Do we sometimes feel left behind? Longing for the beauty we know will come again? Clinging to the memory of a place not quite forgotten? Perhaps the crane is the embodiment of our faith. It returns and remains and waits with a mystical understanding.

Sophie and Teddy walk almost on tiptoe as we creep along the beaches of the barren bay. Even their breath seems hushed.

Together, in unspoken bond, we crouch low and sit and wait – in silence and hope, in low-clinging mist.

We sit and we wait with the crane.

The Easter Parade.

*This afternoon's parade, in the heart of downtown, featured primarily
a host of decked-out doggies.*

It was, indeed, a proper Easter parade. There were fancy bonnets and flowers, streamers and floats. Antique carriages and carts. A grand procession of finery and fun.

In addition to dogs, there were horses as well – some of them tiny miniatures. And a couple of extremely opinionated cats. But all-in-all, the day belonged to the canine set.

It was a fine day for a parade – especially one made up of furry creatures of all sizes, ages and descriptions. Warm in the bright sun, but a cooling breeze to ruffle floppy ears and tails. A fine day.

This day our walk was downtown, to take in all the festivities. When we reached our destination, Sophie and Teddy were almost overwhelmed by all the wondrous possibilities. There were so many people and other dogs and kids who knew how to pet gently. There were smells to smell, and soft wet noses to greet, and tails that said "hello" with enthusiasm.

Everyone was walking and waiting and looking up and down the street, anxious for the parade to begin. And here it came!

"Sophie, sit," I said, "Teddy, stand." (His woefully stiff back legs supercede the sit command for him.)

Sophie reacted immediately and her eyes grew big as the horse-drawn carriages passed right in front of us.

Teddy was facing backward, so he missed that part.

People waved and called out names. Many even commented on how well behaved Sophie was, sitting so calmly. (I knew that, secretly, she was actually rather overcome with awe and thinking that if she sat very still, no one would notice her.)

Teddy still hadn't determined which way to look. Apparently the crowd behind us – or perhaps it was something in the store windows – seemed to be most compelling. His tail was still pointed toward the parade. "Turn around, Ted," I encouraged. But his feet remained firmly planted.

I had to laugh as the assorted dog-borne Easter bonnets became tilted across an ear or slid down the parade participant's back. Many were worn more as ascots than hats. But the idea was there, the festive appearance undaunted.

Sophie never moved. Her ears stayed close to her head. She was fascinated, but sat as close as she could to my legs.

"Teddy, turn around, dear," I kept coaxing. "Look at the doggies … see the horses. Hey, Ted, *cats!*"

But Teddy was in his own unexplained world. Focused on the backside of the parade route. Could he be watching the reflections? I wondered. Or maybe it's a silent "protest" against dogs in hats. (On second thought, that would be a bit sophisticated for my dear Teddy-boy. And probably an unlikely gesture from a dog who wears a cardboard birthday cone on his head with an elastic string under his chin for hours and seems to enjoy it.)

It was a short parade. But exceedingly fun. Full of as much joy for the marchers as it was for the audience.

As we wandered slowly back toward home, I kept wondering what Sophie and Teddy had made out of the whole experience. Was it something they would remember? Was it fun for them, too? Why wouldn't Teddy turn around?

Then I thought perhaps it's like most things in our spiritual lives: some of us are participants, some of us are observers, and some of us let the parade pass us by.

The Face of God.

It rained all through the night. There are cool leftover pools of it
all along our walking route in the horse district this morning.

The day promises early warmth. The rain-glistened grass and leaves are already quivering dry in a gentle breeze; fresh blossoms are releasing their share of moisture into a softly transparent, scented mist.

We've reached the polo practice field and Sophie gleefully accepts her freedom from the leash. Her eyes tell me where she is headed even before she dashes on her way. A quick glance and wink over her shoulder. Two joyful leaps. And then a slow, slooshy slide into her favorite mud pond on the far side of the field. I learned long ago to accept this inevitable treat for her. All of her wide mix of breeds were born under the water sign it seems.

Teddy will have none of it, of course. He prefers to hover at the edge, closely watching over her.

I have noticed that this pond is particularly special to Sophie. She may splash and jump and tap-dance her way through others. But this one is used for a sort of reverent slide and soak only.

Its muddy bottom swirls to the surface around her in milk chocolate clouds gliding across and over and around the ebony base. She watches as her slightest shift creates more of these abstract designs all around her body. She stretches out fully, squishing herself deeper into its coolness. She lowers her head and floats it at chin level – letting a gritty sip slip across the tip of her tongue. She breathes in deeply. A dark, earthy, brown scent. Wet green grasses at the edge add their own colors to the smell.

I watch the watercolor swirls, too – like nature's paint pot – and I see the sun skip across its surface in a dazzling ballet. And I remember. From more than five decades past, the memories are still present and strong.

It was my first earth-born glimpse of God.

At perhaps the age of four, we lived in a house that had a delightful alley shared by the backyards of two blocks of neighbors. Unpaved, it, too, produced some of the most enviable mud puddles after a rain.

As if it were yesterday, I remember tossing pebbles into one exceptionally dark, rich pool. And, as the clouds of light brown rippled upward and swirled in beauty, it caught at my heart. "This is what God looks like," I knew instantly.

I had always been taken to Sunday school. I had looked at and been read to from Bible storybooks. I had seen the paintings and drawings of Jesus framed on the walls (always, it seemed to me, hung much too high up to be studied properly by preschool-height eyes). But here, in this collection of God's own earth and rain, I was seeing God's real image.

I remember that my older sister was nearby. But I didn't call to her. She was older, after all. Perhaps she would already have forgotten. But I knew. I just knew. I remembered.

Today, it comes back to me in a wash of emotion. The image of God. The essence of God. The face of God.

When we are so young – so fresh from God, as Dickens eloquently stated – isn't it just possible that we can still remember Him? Can we still see His face and recognize His reflection and being? And doesn't it somehow seem rather appropriate that it should be found in such an unexpected and humble place? Perhaps also within the souls of God's own dogs the image can be recognized as well.

This morning, I also think about the times when I want desperately to immerse myself in God completely. I want to clasp my knees and cannonball into Him. To stretch out and feel His love and grace squish through my fingers and toes and lap across the tip of my tongue. I want to breathe Him in deeply.

Now, Sophie moves slowly and rises – and God's face disappears and settles back into a cool pond of earthly elements.

She is completely refreshed. She leaps with joy and dances on her back in the grass. She shakes and throws bits of her experience into the air and out to us. She laughs her dog laugh. I suspect she hears the laughter of God along with her.

I envy Sophie her deeply intimate embrace with God this morning. Perhaps it is her innocence that allows the experience.

I wonder if I will find mine again. Will I once more be able to discern the face of God in a mud puddle?

Perhaps, this morning, I did.

The Next Generation.

Something moves on the other side of the gnarled old magnolia tree.
A flash of white. Shifting figures. Faint voices.
Then "clack-clack" – wood against wood. I recognize the sound.

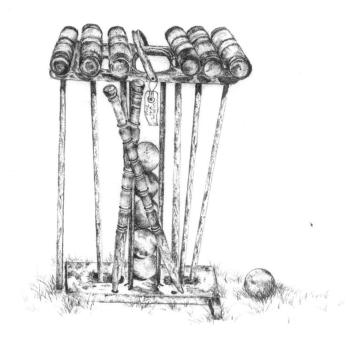

Sophie and Teddy and I are walking one of our typical routes down a well-worn dirt road, which at one point passes along the wooded backside of a private local supper and social club.

It is quite a proper Southern club with gracious manners, an outstanding chef, a lovely old multistoried mansion, and grounds that spread well-kept lawns over several long blocks. Trees abound.

And across the back lawn of the property, just beyond the magnolias and thicket of bushes edging the road, is a permanently maintained croquet field – rolled and watered and pampered just so.

"Sophie, Teddy, wait," I ask in slightly more than a whisper.

We slow our steps and stop just opposite a narrow clearing. We watch silently the scene that is playing out before us.

Everyone is dressed in traditional whites. Young people, who look no more than 10 or 12 years of age, are paired with gray-haired instructors. They are learning the art of the game of croquet.

Rules are carefully being explained; techniques are being patiently practiced. Quietly. With appropriate dignity. But not without just enough giggles, too. There are spectators sitting unobtrusively in dark green lawn chairs at the sides of the field. It is a gentle step out of time. And it makes me smile deeply.

"It's the next generation," I think. "A new generation of civility and tradition."

The lawn itself is cool green and glistening in the morning sun. The children of many ages and genders and races are listening intently, respectfully. The elder players are kind, obviously enjoying the passing on of this centuries-old game to the younger ones.

How much this is like our faith, I consider. One generation to the next. Taught with care; learned with respect. Practiced with patience and gentleness and love.

We have to love what we pass on, I think.

I look over at Sophie and Teddy where they are busily sniffing the ground together. (The game of croquet has ceased to hold any attraction for them.) And I remember how lost Teddy once was. How unaware. How alone. Sophie taught him love. With patience and kindness and unwavering persistence, she led him into play, lifted him into lightheartedness. She helped him find trust. And through it, he learned to have "faith." Faith that no one would hurt him anymore. Faith that he would not be abandoned again.

Sophie has just found a particularly good scent and invites Teddy to share it. She has such a giving heart. I wonder if I represent my faith as completely and well as this singular, loyal creature does.

Suddenly, there is applause from the croquet field. It draws me from my wandering thoughts. What fun it would be if we could "applaud" when faith is passed from one hand to the next.

Perhaps that is, after all, what the passing of faith is supposed to be. Grace and love. One hand to the next. One heart to the next. Encouraging a new generation on its own journey.

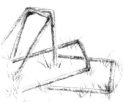

She Looked After The Losers.

It was a small, simple plaque, only about three inches high by five inches long.

It was attached to the back of a plain wood and wrought iron park bench, which stood alone along an out-of-the-way path at the far east side of the city's public gardens. I don't know why it caught my eye. But there it was. Perhaps the sun moved across it just right. The tiny plaque said, quite simply: *"She Looked After The Losers."*

Sophie and Teddy and I had decided that it was too hot to walk anywhere else. But it was wonderfully shady and cool and quiet in this lovely retreat. Usually, Sophie can't wait to watch the fountains. Teddy must see the ducks. We tug anxiously along the brick-lined pathways. This day, it was a slower pace somehow. And I saw it as we passed. *"She Looked After the Losers."*

Her name was also engraved upon the plaque above the statement – Anne Choate Dodd. I didn't recognize it. I don't know anyone of that surname. And yet, I knew something of great importance about Anne Choate Dodd: *She looked after the losers.*

My walkmates would not stop for long. Ducks to the right. Fountains to the left. But the words came with me. They tumbled through my head for the rest of the day. I loved the straightforwardness of them. *"She looked after the losers."*

In our politically correct society, it was refreshing. She did not look after the disadvantaged, or the people who made wrong decisions. She looked after the *losers.* The ones that *lost.* The ones who *were* lost. At least she considered them as having tried. You can't lose if you don't try.

I also appreciated that she "looked after" them. It was active, personally involved, but not condescending. She didn't just care about them. She also didn't take care of them. She looked after them – a subtle difference. And a somehow very Southern way – a very faith-based way – of phrasing it. Anne Choate Dodd looked after the losers.

I brought the dogs back the next afternoon, too. I wanted to see it again, write it down exactly right. I brought a human friend with me this time as well, and we talked about it. She didn't recognize the name either. We wondered aloud about who gave this bench in Anne's memory. Whose lives did she touch so deeply that they would honor her in such an insightful and honest way?

Fate prevented me from having to search very long for the answers. In a chance conversation, I was told that Anne Choate Dodd was the mother of a long-time resident of our small town, someone I knew only slightly at the time – mostly by reputation. And it did not surprise me that this woman of character would have been the daughter of another woman of such obvious substance and character.

I learned that Anne Choate Dodd lived a long and very full life looking after the losers. She took her young daughter with her to visit prison inmates and the mentally ill and others who were sick and down and out. She tucked strangers under her wing and supported the weak and gave money to those who needed it and read the Bible to those who needed it. It was just what she did. She hired a yardman named David who let the lawn fall into woeful neglect and disarray. But when asked, she replied: "Well, honey, you know David's blind."

It wasn't until the daughter was well into her teens that one day she challenged her mother's approach to life. With innocent logic and sense of purpose, her mother responded: "Well, honey, somebody has to look after the losers."

How Jesus-like, I thought. How beautifully, simply, wonderfully, she had followed his example. In so many ways, his entire ministry on earth was spent "looking after the losers." The instructions he left for us were a variation on this singular theme. Love one another. Look after one another. Especially the least among us. And Anne Choate Dodd did just that.

I also learned that this woman of the Word had suffered her own deep losses. Life losses that could crumble most of us. But she was forever full of hope, filled with joy and light and duty – looking after the losers.

When Anne Choate Dodd died, her daughter spoke about her philosophy at her funeral. She built her mother's eulogy around it. She paid tribute to her mother's memory with her own words. Soon after that, a loving nephew donated the bench to the gardens in the mother's honor. The plaque with its words of remembrance was attached.

I know Sophie and Teddy and I will walk by this place often now. Perhaps we will rest awhile on her bench. And I will remember Anne Choate Dodd and feel glad that she lived.

And perhaps one day I will see someone else there, too – reading her legacy. Perhaps it will be someone else's mother, and she will be saying to her own little girl:

"Well, honey … somebody has to look after the losers."

Plans And Possibilities.

It was pure frustration. Sophie was grabbing mouthfuls of grass and flinging them right and left.

Sophie wasn't eating the grass, or digging into the ground. She was ripping the blades off and shaking her head from side to side. She was simply frustrated. And this was her none-too-subtle, passive-aggressive way of letting me know about it.

Sophie, Teddy and I were on our daily walk. We were in the horse district. Down one of the most lovely of its lanes, which is draped in thick, cool shade trees, is the cottage of one of our human friends. This day, we stopped to call on her. She invited us to sit out on the front lawn in comfortable ironwork chairs, surrounded with curtains of climbing roses and bundles of tall sweet oregano. It was a lovely visit. We talked of dogs and horses and books and God and hometowns and houses and farms from long ago.

Sophie and Teddy were gracious and patient, lying at our feet. Listening. Wandering just a bit. Not complaining. Not asking to move on.

Eventually, with a pocket full of fresh-picked aromatic seasoning, I called my walkmates together to continue on our journey.

Just a short way farther down the lane, we came upon another friend. She was feeding her horses, dropping fresh green hay over the sides of newly painted paddock fencing. She called to us, and we again stopped our walk to say "hello" and talk awhile. There was a new barn to admire. And training techniques to discuss. And saving horses from injury, and renewing their lives after sport. The time began to slip away, standing there watching a tall handsome horse enjoy his new hay and extra company.

It was then that I felt Sophie shaking her head at the end of her leash. It was then that I noticed her tossing the grass to one side and then the other. She bent low and ripped another mouthful from the ground and expelled it with force and fury. She was undeniably – and understandably – frustrated that yet another interruption was interfering with our intended walk. No barking. No pulling me along with discourtesy. She chose instead to rip and fling grass in silent protest.

It made me laugh. It also made me excuse us from our visit and continue with the walk.

"Sorry, Sophie," I said. "I know the feeling." And yet, I began to think, there had been plenty for her to enjoy. Horses to nuzzle. Other dogs with whom she could have had a good romp. Different smells to explore. Even a quiet nap could have been taken in the shade. But her mind and heart had apparently been set on the walk experience.

"Dear God," I whispered. "Is this what I do to you? It this how I seem to you when you interrupt my own plans for how I think things should be going?" In my heart, I realized that God must see my silly expressions of frustration as equally amusing. And, I suspect, I may be missing the same kinds of intriguing opportunities that are being presented instead.

"God, help me to see the options you may be offering when you turn me from my focused path," I prayed as we continued our walk down the dirt-packed lane. "Help me to see not the interruptions, but the possibilities."

My Brother's Teacher.

Sophie sits. I'm trying to teach Teddy how to sit. With every command
I give to Teddy, however, Sophie sits.

Sophie actually mastered the act of sitting on command
ages ago. Two lessons, down cold. With Teddy, it's on the scale
of quantum physics. He tries so hard to understand. But this is
simply eluding him.

*Sometimes, I think my faith came easy. But perhaps it
only seems that way in retrospect. I was raised in the church,
but I questioned all its principles and teachings for years in my
early adulthood. I remember struggling with even the most
basic beliefs. I quit going to church. Living a proper life and
doing good was all I needed. Until God sought me out and
brought me home and sat me down and said, "pay attention."*

"Teddy, sit," I say as I pull up a bit on his collar and
press gently but firmly on his rump. Teddy grumbles and
squirms and looks up at me as if I were trying to do him some
great bodily harm. His knees lock. His whole body stiffens.
His nostrils flare. We're not going down without a struggle.

I try the trick of pushing my knees in behind Teddy's – the way we used to do in the hallways of grade school to make someone's legs collapse. Hilarious at 12 years old. Not terribly amusing to a dog – or instructive. It ends in him flopping on top of me in a dead weight and then scrambling with legs and toenails flying to regain his footing. All the while, Sophie keeps sitting quite nicely.

When I was brought back into the fold by God, He started from the beginning. All the basics. I got involved in a Bible study group. I don't exactly know how. I signed a sheet of paper stating that I might be interested in hearing more about the class, and the next thing I knew, I was told I was bringing refreshments. Popcorn would be fine, thank you very much.

When I first found Teddy, he was in pitiable condition. He had been chained or tied to something for so long, his back legs were weak and underdeveloped. His joints were stiff and painful. At the age of just four years, he was an old man. A broken spirit.

Today, he is still an "old soul." But good nutrition and
exercise and medical care have brought him renewed health.
Sophie has given him new life. It was she who gave him his will
to live.

Most of us in my first Bible study class were
"beginners." Some had childhood experiences, such as mine.
Others came from an upbringing with an absolute absence of
spirituality. We all had so much to learn, such a long way to
go. Our journey was just starting. But we shared with one
another openly, freely, honestly. It was a very safe place to be.
We were traveling together, as brothers and sisters.

As soon as Teddy entered our home, Sophie devoted
herself to him. She urged and nagged and coaxed him to play,
although he did not know even this most basic of behaviors.
She would not give up. At first, they "dog wrestled" lying down
– because Teddy's back legs were so weak he would have fallen
over if they had been standing. As he grew in strength, she
teased him into running games. She tackled him, rolled him,
wrestled him to the ground over and over again, until he began
to be able to hold his own.

Now, on our daily walks, he trots at equal speed, runs
without pain, keeps pace with the other dogs. Typically he is the
last one, but he never gives up.

*My brothers and sisters in spirit have wrestled me to
the ground on occasion. They also started where I needed to
begin. With no more than I could handle. Gentle prodding.
Sweet good humor. Celebration with each new concept
understood, each step forward. As my faith grew stronger,
the challenges from my spiritual family grew, too. "Take it into
the world," they whispered. "Live in the world, but not of it,"
they urged.*

Sophie and Teddy and I usually practice our obedience
training out in the open polo field, where the grass is soft and
the sun is warm and the mood is light. And, admittedly, where
Teddy's distractions are great. It's a good test, out in reality,
I reason.

Sophie actually believes obedience training is a performance art, after all. Always best with an audience. But with Teddy, it's a deep and personal struggle to understand. He wants so desperately to understand. Because with understanding comes belonging. And Teddy wants nothing so much as to belong to us and with us. Unconditional love is so new to him. I strive for him to develop his fledgling sense of entitlement. I want him to believe that he is worthy of love simply because he is Teddy. Simply because he is.

Over the years since I came back to "belonging" to a church family – a family of faith – I have moved across congregations and denominations and towns and states. But now I know that I always belong to the family of God. I am a child of God. With this understanding, my faith continues to mature. It has settled into my heart. I have settled into my faith. And still I am determined not to lose my awe of discovery. My heart must always keep its enthusiasm to learn; its ability to be overwhelmed with God's grace. All the while, every step I move forward, my faith family never fails to call out to me: "Good job. Well done."

"Teddy, sit," I say again, with encouragement strong in
my voice. And, again, Sophie sits. And now I see it. I realize
how Sophie is purposefully walking *in front* of Teddy before
she responds to the command. She is quite deliberately *showing*
him what to do. She is demonstrating by her own actions. She
is teaching her brother by example.

*By example, my brothers and sisters in faith are
my teachers. By example, they ask me to live and be in
the world. This Christianity cannot be a "performance
art." It must be a way of life, in life.*

Once again, the wisdom of dogs is brought home to me.
Live by example. Love by actions. Writer George Eliot once
said: "What do we live for, if not to make life less difficult for
each other?" Perhaps this is the God lesson I am meant to be
learning. Perhaps Sophie is doing just that. And Teddy sits.

The Breath Of God.

"Be still, and know that I am God."

I breathed out fully and into the soft, warm, moist nostrils of a large chestnut horse. He stood stiff and on edge. Ready to bolt.

"Be still and know that I am." I inhaled the animal's breath deeply into myself. I caught and matched his pace of breathing. It was too fast, too strong, over excited.

"Be still and know that I am." I exhaled into him over and over, and began to slow his breathing to meet my own. He relaxed his neck and brought his muzzle closer to me. I still did not touch him with my hands.

"Be still and know." We continued our exchange of breath, slower and softer, slower and softer.

"Be still." His eyes were half closed. Without moving, he allowed the halter to be slipped over his head, the rope looped across his nose.

We spoke then in low voices. "Good boy. Be still. Good boy." His owner led him quietly back to the barn. I turned the other way, left the paddock, and retrieved Sophie and Teddy from beneath the shade tree where they had been tied and waiting for the past several minutes.

Breathing up a horse's nose is not a new technique of calming and communicating with the animal. And, it certainly isn't anything I discovered on my own. I remember hearing it mentioned first by Barbara Woodhouse, an extraordinary English woman who was perhaps the original dog and horse whisperer. But I have greatly enjoyed the experience of using it whenever I meet a horse. It is, after all, their own preferred greeting. And breathing the scripture passage from Psalm 46:10, *"Be still and know that I am (God),"* as a form of prayerful meditation, has always calmed my own spirit. And so, it seems, it does the same for God's other creatures.

Sophie, Teddy and I were about halfway through our walk this particular day in the horse district. We had traveled past a rather small paddock where a large, handsome stallion was running wildly from side to side. He stopped occasionally to look at the man with the halter and lead in his hand. He kicked and even reared with defiance. The man was patient, quietly approaching him. The horse was having none of it.

"Can I help?" I offered.

"Probably not," the man replied. "He's just full of himself and this is a game to him. He'll get tired of it."

And so, we walked on.

On our return trip past this same paddock, however, the scene was still being played out. This time, there was also a woman assisting the man in trying to capture the wayward animal. This time, I simply tied the dogs to a tree in the shade and, uninvited, stepped into the paddock.

The horse spotted me immediately. Someone new. A different stance. A different scent. He came closer to check me out. I began breathing up his nose, arms at my sides. He was intrigued and joined in the greeting. From there, we progressed into relaxation and breath prayers: *"Be still and know that I am."*

How beautiful that gift is from God. That ultimate, absolute reassurance and promise. It reaches across lines of culture, experience, faith, and even species.

"Be still and know that I am." I wonder if, in the beginning, this is how God gave man the breath of life. He stood near. Without touching. Breathed deeply into us. Took our breath into himself. Perhaps this is the way each new life continues to begin. Perhaps it is how each life is completed.

I was incredibly at peace as I returned home that day. The dogs sensed the mood and echoed it in their own quiet, contemplative pace. With every step, God's rhythm was our own.

"Be still and know that I am."

Of Fish And Sandals And Ponds.

It is achingly hot. The air is thick and sticky and slow.

We choose the public gardens for our walk today. In search of deep shade and cool ponds.

In this breathless heat, my walkmates move slowly, too. A good opportunity to examine single blades of grass and smooth brown leaves and soft dust beneath our toes and damp scents on the breath of small breezes.

We stop at the apex of a short bridge over a manmade brook. Looking down, I see wondrous fish. They are like those remembered from childhood, kept on a bedside table in a round glass bowl with marbles lining the bottom. They are bright orange and white with black spots. Some have all three colors dappled across their backs. But these fish are immense. Two feet long at least. They rise and slide effortlessly near the sparkle of the surface.

"Sophie, Teddy," I call. "Look. Look there in the water." I want them to see and enjoy this marvel. But pointing means nothing to Teddy, who closely examines my finger.

I toss small pebbles into the pond near the miracle fish. Sophie does better and tries to look in the direction I am leading her. But her gaze catches at the water's edge, the ripple on the surface, the rocks that protrude. Neither of them can see beneath the surface, past that defining line that separates the elements of air and water.

Parables, I wonder? Is this like the parables Jesus brought us? He laid it all before us to see. He pointed to them unmistakably. And some of us saw only as far as the end of his hand. A few saw further. But still not below the surface, not beyond the reality that surrounds us, that binds us to this earth.

What are those marvels Jesus wanted us to know – just out of sight, just out of reach, just beyond understanding? The shimmering reflections of our reality still distract us from their deeper message. But perhaps that is their ultimate purpose after all. I wonder if all we are supposed to know is that there is more. Beyond what we can know, there is more. And once, there was a man who loved us so much, he tried to show us, tried to teach us how to see beyond, beneath and through our human limitations.

Sophie and Teddy plod along beside me now as we move to a smaller, shallower stream. Sophie steps into it without hesitation. She glides her feet slowly along the cool water's stream. I join her, sandals and all. Teddy reluctantly, trustingly, ultimately comes along.

They could not share the wonder I tried to show them in the deeper, richer, wonder-filled waters. And so I walk with them in theirs.

Was this what Jesus did for us? Perhaps it was. Sandals and all.

Deliver Us From Evil.

Down one nearby sun-washed dirt-packed road, on the far side of
a plain painted fence, hidden behind some thick green bushes,
dwells a pure definition of "temptation and evil."

It's disguised within the body of one large brown dog.

Slobbery mouth, loud bark, terrifying growl, this is the whole package. He sits and waits. He lurks. It's what temptation and evil often do.

Being the consummate lover of dogs, I cannot swear to the fact that this shorthaired canine pet is, in fact, the personification of evil. Perhaps in a one-to-one meeting alone, he may show his kinder, gentler self. Although I know evil can often take on that appearance as well. It isn't always all teeth and snorts and confrontation. It can sneak up on soft toes and compliments.

But my opinion aside, Sophie and Teddy are quite convinced that this particular animal is the poster-dog for absolute evil and temptation. They know it with the kind of conviction that children know the monsters that live in the dark side of the closet, with the same certainty that mothers have about no good happening to a teenager after 2:00 in the morning.

On our walks into the horse district, I would prefer to not even pass through this particular place of temptation and evil, but it is inevitable. It's the primary path. The most direct route. And, most days, we can walk unnoticed by the beast. But we are always alert.

Today, we are taking this path, and Sophie has her standard preparation. Still half a block away, she begins to kick up dirt with her back legs. She shakes out her fur to full depth. She gives off low growls. As we approach the fence, she faces it squarely, grits her teeth, hops past it sideways with stiffened legs. Rephrasing a Biblical passage from Isaiah 47, I can imagine her taking off her veil, lifting up her skirts, baring her legs, and wading through the streams.

All femininity set aside, her paws are fairly clenched and ready to take vengeance and spare no one.

I must note that Sophie is one of the best peacemakers I know. A loving dog who can bring a sense of fun and joy to any situation, and coax it from the hearts of most animals and humans alike. A player of games, who includes one and all. She insists on a level field, allowing large and small, old and young, of all species, equal opportunity to participate. She is a true example of Christian principles. But she will also never back down from a fight. She takes all comers. And, I might add, holds her own admirably when necessary.

Teddy, on the other hand, believes in keeping his head down, avoiding eye contact, and pretending nothing is happening. If confronted directly, he will look away and metaphorically put his paws to his ears while singing "la-la-la-la-la." Move on ... move quickly. Hear no evil, see no evil, there is no evil.

As I watch my two life examples, my own "Teddy-ness" embarrasses me. I cringe at missed opportunities to stand firm against evil and injustice. I wish I could react with the kind of proactive courage and instinct that Sophie exhibits.

Somehow, my mind turns to the Lord's Prayer passage: *"Lead us not into temptation, but deliver us from evil."* Both seem so passive to me. Until I realize that they seem to refer only to the temptation and evil that affect "us" – not our friends or other human beings or creatures. The prayer seemingly asks for guidance only away from the temptation that I may be led into, personally ... the evil that I may find surrounding me alone. Is that significant, I wonder?

On occasion, the big brown "evil" dog does come lunging out at us from behind the bush, and I do prefer it when Sophie lets me handle it alone. A firm voice, a meaningful hand motion, a "no" with conviction, and big brown turns away sputtering. I do not need Sophie's help. Perhaps God doesn't need mine. Perhaps the many sputtering impotent "lunges" of evil in life that are directed at us personally do not need more than God's intervention. Perhaps "deliver us from evil" is a prayer for humility and patience. A prayer to acknowledge that I do not, must not, control all things. I must not seek my own vengeance. I must wait for God to deliver me.

As we reach the far edge of the place where "temptation and evil" reside, Teddy has yet another habitual and ritualistic response. He relieves himself in a spot where big brown dog can surely detect it. Where big brown dog can be sorely tempted to become aggressive.

Another "aha" moment. Perhaps "lead us not into temptation" is also a prayer for my own actions. May I not *be* the temptation, the passive-aggressor. Please God, lead my heart away from doing what is sure to provoke evil in others.

"Lead us not into temptation, but deliver us from evil." The words have more compelling possibilities for me now. More contemplative options.

By now, of course, both Sophie and Teddy have moved on completely. Always in the moment, the "now" of life.

Evil is pouting behind us.

Temptation is drying up in the wind.

God Must Have A Dog.

Peewee. Peep-O. Minx. Tiny. Lily. My Kim.

Their small brick-shaped granite grave markers are aged and edged in black. Some are sunken unevenly into the ground. Others stand high. One is marble, still white, but dated almost half a century in the past. The others have no indication of time.

They are spaced carefully near one another. Placed with obvious precision and love. In remembrance of one family's animal friends from generations ago. They confirm to me the ageless, timeless, infinite bond between dogs and cats and other creatures and us humans.

Sophie first discovered these tiny headstones at the far southeast corner of the fountains in the now public gardens near our home. Once a private residence that entertained princes and dukes and presidents and other notables of society, the grounds were transferred to the city with civic-minded generosity, and are maintained today with the same spirit of love and respect.

I had heard tales of the small pet memorial ground, but had never been able to find it within these park-like acres. Today, Sophie has drawn us to it, and I read the names aloud to us all. I try to imagine them in life.

Tiny ... He must have been small of stature but, I imagine, probably huge in personality and self-image and heart.

Peep-O ... Another small creature, perhaps a bird, who sang or pretended to talk and kept secrets ever so well.

Minx ... Scrappy and proud and smart, I suspect, with an unequalled joy of life.

Peewee ... This little one I think was shy and slow to trust. But once his heart was given, there was no taking it back. Loyal to the end.

Lily ... Most likely as sweet and lovely as the blossom after which she was named. A pampered lady, but never one to let it go to her head.

My Kim ... So loved, I believe, she belonged to no one but her mistress. She chose her human with every inch of her heart, leaving no room for anyone else.

As I try to see the images in my mind of these much-loved creatures, with only their names left behind to suggest their physical beings to me, I am reminded of my unhesitating belief that all animals are endowed with a soul. That they are, indeed, with us in heaven. I have no proof, of course; but I do have utter faith in it being so.

Animals are, after all, all about energy. They feel and sense and are directed by it far beyond our human capabilities, with tremendous intuition and nuance. And what are our souls, I wonder, except the essence of energy?

Perhaps our animals allow us this debate of the presence of soul as yet one more opportunity to have and express our faith. It seems to me that God has given us these creatures on earth to love and be loved unconditionally. His own example of the meaning of love. Why, then, would we suppose that we are so far superior to them that only we as humans will live beyond this earthly existence?

I believe with all my heart that God will hold my beloved animals in the safety of his hand until I may, again, hold them in my arms. And so, with complete and unquestioning faith, I will now also look forward to one day greeting Tiny, Peep-O, Minx, Peewee, Lily and My Kim.

Teddy Got His Butt Blessed.

Teddy got his butt blessed on Palm Sunday afternoon.
It was a lovely ceremony.

The loveliness was not in the blessing of Teddy's hindquarters, per se, but the entire Blessing of the Animals that was hosted by First Presbyterian Church in the center of town. It was an inaugural event for the church, and one I personally hope will continue on an annual basis.

The sun was warm on the west lawn of the church. There were folding chairs and blankets spread on the ground. People came from every direction and every denomination. There was music and refreshments, prayers and celebration. It was a very spiritual experience.

Those who came to be blessed were mostly dogs of every description, a few slightly startled cats, at least one goldfish that I knew about. Everyone was quite congenial and reverent. There was a deep sense of peace throughout the gathering. So I'm not sure why Teddy refused to willingly participate.

There had been heavy storms the night before, and he continues to be deeply affected by some past, private terror related to such weather. Perhaps he was still wary from it. And the music was live and rather loud. And there were strangers all around. And Sophie was quite the social butterfly, working the room, and perhaps not as attentive to him as he would have wished.

I had to be away from him during much of the event, too – helping to serve communion and other duties.

So Teddy's solution was to make himself as tiny as possible, and climb backwards under my folding chair. His tail tucked tightly against his body. His limbs curled against himself. His head down. Pretending he wasn't even there. Only his backside protruded from the front of the seat ever so unobtrusively.

After the singing and prayers and special remarks, the humans were offered communion. Walking immediately behind the servers, the minister for the event came to each animal and blessed him or her individually. First one row, then the next. Touching each creature personally with love and tenderness. Asking God's blessing on each small soul.

Sophie accepted her blessing with a light heart and happy spirit. Then, it was Teddy's turn. I could only glimpse bits of what was going on, as I was serving communion and focused more on the duties at hand. But at Teddy's chair, the minister paused longer than usual. She was kneeling on the ground. Coaxing. Encouraging. Gently prodding. But Ted was refusing to respond.

Ever since I took Teddy in to live with Sophie and me, I have had to accept that Teddy is going to do what Teddy is going to do. He has come a long way from his early days of abject fear and mistrust. But he will, at times, retreat into himself and simply refuse a new experience. Often unexpectedly. Always irretrievably. This was such a moment.

I am grateful to the Reverend for her persistence, and ultimate acceptance. She simply blessed what she could reach of him. And Teddy got his butt blessed.

Perhaps we are all "Teddys" at some times in our lives. Perhaps we, too, refuse to leave our hiding places, our comfort zones, our self-designed invisibility. And, in doing so, I wonder what delights we forego, what blessings we miss receiving?

I hope we are all fortunate enough to have someone in our lives who will coax us, encourage us, prod us. And, when all else fails, asks God to bless our butts anyway.

Living The Mystery.

"What were you thinking?"

As Sophie returns from a rebellious run after a squirrel at the edge of a tree-lined field, I can't help but question her out loud. "What *were* you thinking?"

She has just dashed, unheeding, across the road from where we are walking. She threw that special glance at me over her shoulder just before she sprinted away, so I knew it was coming. It was in total defiance – with complete disregard for commands to "wait" or "stop" or "stay" or "sit."

These breaks in training and manners are infrequent. And, typically, there are squirrels involved. And the wayward romps always result in the same reattachment of the leash – a loss of freedom on her part. And yet, it is as if she weighs the temptation against the punishment and opts for the few minutes of unbridled chase, regardless of the consequence.

I wish I could explain to her the full and true potential consequences of such decisions. The danger of the road. The unseen car or horse or unfriendly dog. The fear I feel in being separated from her, perhaps losing her completely.

There is an old folktale that tells about the magic of Christmas Eve, when, just at the stroke of midnight, the animals can speak. I have often contemplated that opportunity with thoughts of things I would say and ask and try to explain with my beloved pets.

How long does this moment of magic last, I wonder? Could I explain about vaccinations and flea treatments and baths? Or should I only concentrate on why rules are necessary and what my commands mean and why just one cookie at a time? If the time were extremely limited, perhaps I should only talk to them of love and friendship and how much they mean to my very heart and soul.

And what would I ask them in return? Why do they bark at sounds too distant for me to even hear? Why does Sophie refuse to sleep on the bed when Teddy is there? Why does Teddy fear abandonment even from me? Do they understand how much I love them, and fear for their safety, and long for their companionship?

What would I ask? What would I say? If only I could find that one magic moment in time.

Most of us spend a great deal of effort in search of God's meanings. We study the teachings of Jesus, the Bible, the wisdom of great writers and thinkers and educators from the ancient past to the progressive now. We may even plead for God to show us his secrets. Perhaps we spend precious time in prayer asking for such answers and insights.

And yet, with the animals, they and I somehow find other ways to communicate. We watch each other's body language and eyes. We learn each other's dislikes and likes by observation and reaction. We laugh and sing and cry together even when each of us laughs and sings and cries differently. We comfort and share our joys simply by "being" one with the other. We trust each other with our hearts. Eventually, we even come to *appreciate* the mysteries between us. We learn to accept those things we cannot truly understand. We live simply in the mystery of the relationship.

I suspect I might benefit greatly if I applied these same principles to my relationship with God. I am, after all, not meant to have all the answers. Perhaps I am meant to live in – and simply enjoy – the mystery.

End Times In The Woods.

The dogs are always slow to enter this part of the woods.

I have used this entrance to our beloved woods countless times, and Sophie and Teddy always react the same. There seems to be such a multitude of compelling sights and scents, calling them to individual leaves and twigs and rocks that look quite ordinary to my eye, but that have complex portraits and multilayered histories to share with well-honed canine senses.

Countless times, I must have also passed by this one particular trail that turns sharply off to the right. It's obviously much less traveled – thinner in width, thicker in ground cover. Just a path, really.

Small yellow buds on bushes and delicate violets against the ground first caught my eye. Then young magnolia trees. It always amazes and delights me how these Southern beauties – so cultivated in demeanor and image – can grow wild in the thickets of the woods. Strong, old, massive, gorgeous. They spread their arms in sassy celebration that they survive well here. Their creamy tactile blossoms always seem to beckon like sultry Southern girls on summer nights – only half innocence and purity. Farther down, red-orange berries also invite us to come their way along the unknown path this afternoon.

I turn Sophie and Teddy toward the new trail and they readily oblige. It is slightly uphill. The thickness hushes the atmosphere behind curtains of trees and vines and undergrowth. And yet, there seem to be more stirrings of unseen wildlife than usual all about us. Another sign of fewer visitors, I suspect. A sudden rustle just ahead. Sophie turns to me with a look of private shared understanding. "Fairies," I whisper back.

There are a few horse hoof prints now as the leaves underfoot slough off to reveal the bare earth beneath. I find this strangely encouraging, somehow. We're not the first to pass this way.

The silence seems to be increasing.

The path winds and twists and comes abruptly to a choice of left or right turns. Sophie and Teddy wait expectantly for me to decide. Both ways curve so sharply it's impossible to see more than a few yards in either direction. Arbitrarily, we turn left. A slight slope downward. Not far, we are stopped suddenly by a huge, steep drop-off. Perhaps a cave in; a giant sinkhole. The pit is terrifyingly deep. The edge is straight down. And yet, Sophie, in her youthful enthusiasm and sense of adventure begins to look for a way down. She is ready to try it, if I allow and urge her to do so.

"No," I caution. "This one's too steep."

Teddy does not even question the possibility. We turn to go in the opposite direction.

We are soon back at our original crossroads. We'll try the other way, we decide. And so we continue. Around corners and turns and twists to an unseen future. This time, slightly uphill.

Gradually, as I allow my gaze to leave the uneven trail long enough to look forward, I see something terribly odd coming into view. It resembles some mythical, skinned creature – or something dinosaur-like – but many times larger. The rib cage is huge and barren and grayish-tan in the open space, the sun illuminates it starkly. It is an utter mystery.

Eventually, we come near it. Still uncertain, we detect a pungent new smell. The dogs hesitate. I recognize this odor. Burnt wood and leaves and earth. Walking forward, we see batches of charred wood bits and thick branches poking up like owls watching us as we come nearer. They remain silent statues while we walk among the heaps and mountains of what seems like molten ash.

The officials and guardians of the woods occasionally have controlled burns, I remember. Perhaps this is where they bring some of the brush to sacrifice. Year after year. Ashes melting over ashes. Rain soaking it to sludge. Wind transforming it to leaden earth. Not quite mud. Not solid. It clings to the soles of my shoes and the dogs' footpads. It's dead here. Silent and gray and stagnant and dead.

As we try to leave, our feet become even more coated with the ashy slush. It makes walking difficult. But there, at the edge, I notice the new growth. Small saplings of pine, just a few inches tall, but green and healthy and plunging toward the sun from this nutrient-rich death.

We walk slowly out to the path. The dogs want to stop and lick their feet. I scrape my shoes and try to help them with their pads, but it sticks and clings and refuses to be removed. I reason if we continue to walk down the path to the main trail, perhaps it will be lost along the way. We return to the cut off and turn down hill. The clay-like substance still coating my soles makes me slip on the loose leaves. The dogs slide, too, with unaccustomed lack of stability.

This is both fascinating and uncomfortable. Compelling and repelling. I am a little afraid. I have glimpsed the end of this trail, and it is enigmatic. One way is an impassible pit. The other is death but resurrection as well. And now, we are bringing it back – clinging to us – into this world.

Is that what the Biblically prophesized "end times" will be like? Will we be allowed to bring the afterlife into this one? Will we know both worlds as one?

Perhaps the idea of "left behind" means the saved will be the ones left behind. Sin will be taken away. And the rest will be allowed re-growth and beauty and life – everlasting yet familiar.

God's mysteries intrigue me. I am sorry I find fear before comfort in them. I hope to grow my faith beyond the fear. I don't know why I can't yet.

But for today, I am glad this symbolic next life material stuck to my feet. I am somehow comforted that it covered the dogs' feet as well as my own.

I sit contemplating this experience on my back steps at home. I am tempted to not clean my shoes.

The Trail Left Behind.

I suspect everyone leaves a trail of some kind in life.

I watch my two canine companions carefully examine the edges of the well-worn dirt roads as we wander through the horse district near our home.

Their styles are completely different when "reading" a trail, I've noticed. Sophie speed-reads her way along, while Teddy thoroughly revels in every individual syllable and nuance.

I am intrigued with how each of them approaches the subject so diversely. Isn't it the same scent? Shouldn't it be communicating the same thing to each of them? We walk these hushed familiar roads almost daily. I would think the scent-messages would not change much. The same walkers and wildlife, repeating their own journeys and daily searches.

What knowledge do the dogs actually gain, I wonder? I suspect it is quite detailed … the passerby's species and size and gender, perhaps its age and health as well. What about temperament and mood and purpose, the rate of travel and direction? Do they recognize repeat visitors? Are there hidden messages for them to discover? Are the layers of scent difficult to discern one from the next?

Just now I detect a sweet familiar fragrance myself. Gardenias, I think. Yes, I see their creamy white blossoms up ahead, radiant against their dark green satin foliage. The lovely aroma washes over me with the breeze. God's scent, I think. God's trail of scent.

How well do I follow God's trail left for me? Jesus walked the path to show me the way. Christ left me the message to discern. But how faithfully do I follow? Sometimes I know I rush past in my speedwalk through life. Perhaps in doing so, I miss too much. Important messages. Intended lessons.

The trails of God are multilayered too, I believe. Sometimes we may look at something day after day, walk after walk; and then, suddenly, we see. I suspect God holds these insights for us until our hearts are ready to receive them.

Sophie and Teddy use their sense of smell as an integral part of their lives. I know, of course, theirs is hundreds of times more acute than mine. It is their second sight, their inherent enabler to a richer life.

But so often, scents enfold me, too. Bringing my childhood to the present. The aroma of a particular soap is my grandfather's memory. Fresh-picked cherries evoke the trees on the family farm where I climbed and scraped my knees and gathered fruit in buckets for grandma and aunt Minnie to bake pies. My mother's perfume on a handkerchief. Old books and blackboard chalk. Wooden churches. New shoes. Sweet puppy breath. And, now, the thick scent of gardenias, to associate with the horse district where I love to walk with dogs. A scent to remind me of beautiful animals, and spiritual musings, and thoughts about and with God.

I wonder, too, about the trails we all must leave behind. Dogs who follow Sophie and Teddy and me on these paths will surely know us. Will people who follow you and me in life know us as well – through our deeds and words, our trails of actions and thoughts? Will our children follow our trail? (Or perhaps they are the trail itself we leave behind.)

I believe I want to make my trail one of kindness and integrity. Of love. Of thoughtful deeds and comforting words. I want the trail I leave behind to be broad and traveled well. I want it to be one walked with dogs and shared with others and remembered after I am gone. I want it to be a trail of written words and encouragement. But most importantly, I am discovering, I want it to be along the same path left by Jesus – with my footsteps following his. Perhaps my trail is meant to refresh and share the message he left behind – if only for one fellow traveler.

The dogs are thirsty now.

We stop to drink,

and turn for home.

God Bless you
and the creatures
you love.

Also By Author Marti Healy

The God-Dog Connection was Marti's first published book and remains one of her most popular works. It is a collection of small, gentle vignettes featuring observations of animal behavior and the faith lessons she draws from them. A lovely companion book to "Walking with Dogs," it takes a slightly different approach to a similar theme (and also includes a number of stories about cats).

The Rythym of Selby, winner of the Bronze Medal for Popular Fiction from the Independent Publishers Awards for excellence and two INDIE Awards for writing and design.

The Secret Child, an Okra Pick by the Southern Independent Booksellers Alliance (SIBA) and DaVinci Eye Award Finalist for the Eric Hoffer Book Awards.

The Childornot Tales, Finalist for the INDIE Next Generation Award.